Our C
Library

Henrietta Lily

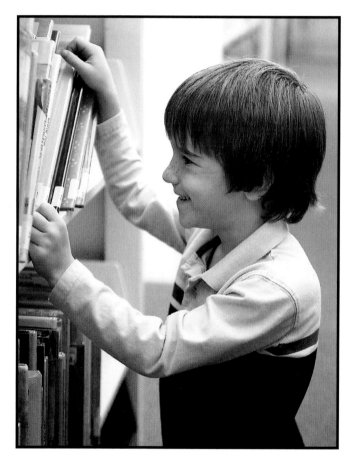

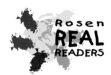

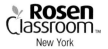

New York

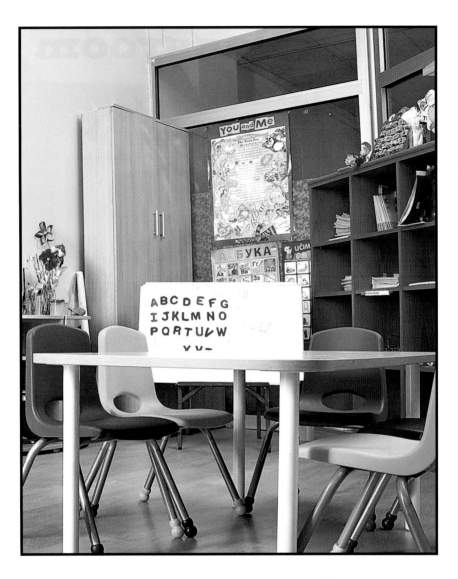

This is our classroom library.

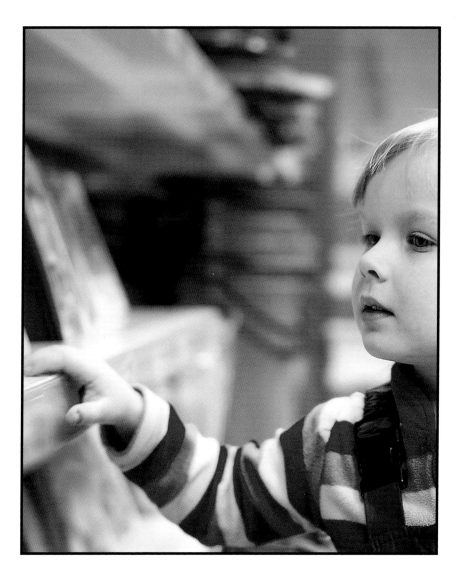

I get a book.

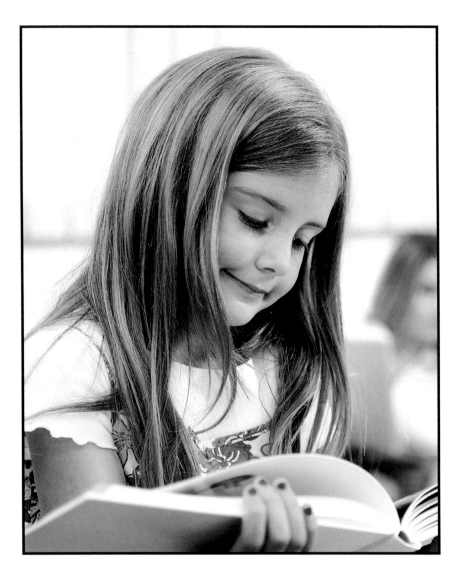

I read a book from our library.

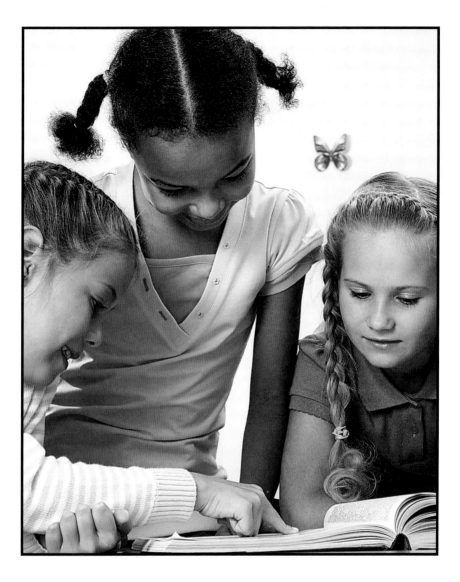

We read a book together.

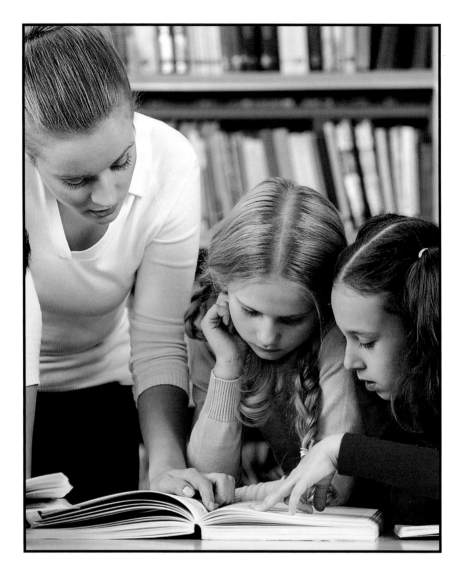

Our teacher helps us read
a book.

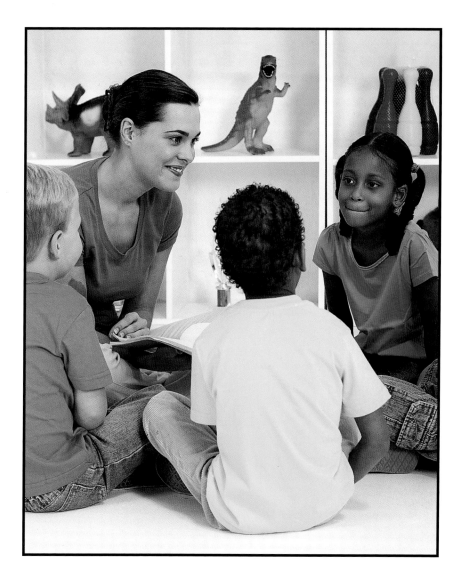

Our teacher reads to us.

Words To Know

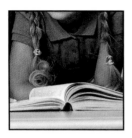

book

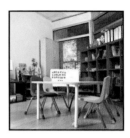

classroom

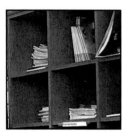

library

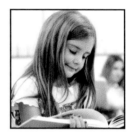

read